Matter of *Time*

SANGEETH MONCY

INDIA • SINGAPORE • MALAYSIA

ISBN
Paperback 979-8-89588-670-0
Hardcase 979-8-89610-335-6

Contents

Writer's Note

The poems in this book, *Matter of Time*, are like tiny dots that come together to form a vivid portrait of myself. This collection weaves together themes of nature, love, satire, and philosophy, each piece reflecting a facet of my journey. Writing these poems has been a joyful experience, allowing me to release my feelings and energy into the universe.

Wordsworth's insight that poetry captures "Emotions recollected in tranquility" relates deeply with me, as does T.S. Eliot's observation of "The greatest poems are not those which most perfectly express the poet's own feelings, but those which most perfectly express the feelings of all men." As time flows, nothing remains final. Poetry is like moving inner illumination, as you know. In many ways, modern man still seeks to connect with the wisdom of the pilgrim souls. My life has traversed turbulent phases, and while I may not share those experiences directly, they are woven throughout these verses.

As a reader, you may find reflections of your own life within these poems. Poetry serves as a powerful medium to express and communicate our emotions to the world. I hope these poems resonate with you and open your heart to new possibilities!

– Sangeeth Moncy

Foreword

I feel glad that there is a recent surge of English writers from Kerala, gaining limelight on both a pan-Indian and global level. The exuberant lineage of modern Kerala writing—initiated by pioneers like Kamala Das and continued by contemporary canonical writers such as Jeet Thayil, C.P. Surendran, Anupama Raju, Babitha Justin, Chandramohan S. and Meera Nair—has carried forth the project of Kerala modernity in a holistic sense. I consider the young and promising poet, Sangeeth Moncy, as a new voice of English poetry from Kerala, following the path set by such a wonderful spectrum of writers. I hold a broad view that modern English poetry is not a mere extension of the traditional trend, which has been extensively celebrated and idealised, but is inspired by technological and cultural upheavals. Sangeeth's poetry shows this kind of an affinity towards a paradigm shift of Kerala writing in English.

In Sangeeth's world, I see cats, birds, crosses, fire, magical rings, and above all, the ever looming presence of an omnipotent power. His genuinely 'happy poems' converse with an imperceptible supreme energy, visible to him in his own way. I find in his work a constant presence of a young child—perhaps a classroom boy—on a quest for peace and harmony of the world. His poetry carries a joyous and blissful note on nature, serving as an ode to his personal experiences and his engagement with everything he is surrounded by.

Sangeeth finds happiness and positivity in the idea of absolute 'creation', and expresses his gratitude towards life in simple yet discreet and direct ways, as in the poems "Ocean of Dreams" and "The Blanket." He praises the amiable appeal of minute natural things and feels:

> "The beauty of everything
> Projects in this nature's blanket.
> Sometimes it changes the scene
> To attract you more." ["The Blanket"]

Often opting for a kind of positivity, Sangeeth tries to find solace in the idea of moving forth, despite hindrances that life attributes. The boundless sanguinity in him—as voiced in his poems—seems to reflect his cheerful memories and experiences. His relentless optimism and hope for the mankind is evident here:

> "The Titanic was blown by ego,
> Leading to a massive failure.
> But it was not the end of dreams;
> We learned from it
> To dream even higher." ["Ocean of Dreams"]

I feel that these poems at times traverse among sleep, wakefulness and complete awareness of everything around. Sangeeth constantly navigates between his dreams and reality, and is often captivated by certain visions that make him ponder over life as on a grander scale. He often believes that dreams would offer him comfort and form the very foundation of his being. He says:

> "Dreams are like tiny sticks
> That fall from the tree of dreams.
> Take time and feel it;
> Dream many
> To make a nest of life." ["To Happen"]

In his constant pursuit for harmony, Sangeeth expresses a belief that "Peace floats everywhere" ["Complete"], while supposing himself as serenely "Floating like a lotus/In a tranquil lake," ["Lotus Left"], inviting readers to a gentle, reflective journey through his work. Apart from that, he seeks delight in the unique profound nature of objects, and reveres the mystical and other-worldly energy that has caused it, as in poems like "Search for Paradise," "The Kingdom" and "Season of Blames." His conversation with the supreme power takes on various forms and moods, from reverence to pleading as in:

> "You saved humanity;
> Else it would be thrashed.
> And you saved me too." ["Time Traveller"]
> "Oh! God, why are you doing this?
> Please save the world." ["Eclipse"]

Sangeeth's epitome of love elevates to a spiritual and platonic dimension, with his transcendent ideologies on human affection and relationships. He experiences the presence of an omniscient spirit in the very creation of his beloved:

"Godly skill reflects on you
As your charm goes on and on." ["The Supreme"]

Besides, the core of Sangeeth's verse sits not on the idea of being static, but on the notion of frequent dynamic changes. Time, on many occasions, becomes a major character and an intimidating entity in his poems like "Autobiography" and "Life is Somewhere." He embraces the whole idea of time, and believes that change is inevitable in the process of human growth. Sangeeth often contemplates the possibility of navigating between the past, present and future as in poems like "Nowhere." He consumes the entire essence of human life in its totality by succumbing himself to the indisputable agency of time. Through the recurring sequential processes of learning, unlearning, and re-learning of the things in life, he proposes a democratic way of living as in the very title of the anthology, *Matter of Time*.

"Now all these experiences
Made the real me
In a matter of time" ["Matter of Time"]

Sangeeth strives to break free from all the shackles hindering freedom, expressing a desire to seek joy amidst all the confusions around. His constant urge to be let open in his world of being a writer becomes explicit in poems like "Bunker," "No More Caged" and "Mr. Perfect." I could experience a sense of autonomy in him when he writes about his longing to live as a carefree artist. He proclaims his freedom and announces that "Life has taught me the value/ Of true freedom, and I rejoice!" ["No More Caged"]. A philosophical undercurrent runs through almost all his poems, and his enthusiasm at times attain a theological tone. Often meditative and introspective by nature, Biblical images and themes set a major tone to his poetry, but in a pleasant yet open fashion.

Significantly enough, Sangeeth's writings are not engulfed in a state of perpetual darkness that often pervades modern poetry. Instead, I feel that this poet with his simple vocabulary, does not intend to jargonise English language but simply longs to articulate and voice his youthful experiences. It is at this point that the genuineness in his poetry I had mentioned earlier, becomes most apparent. Candid and innocent in his own way, it is too early and not so easy to foresee the trajectory he will take as a poet.

I would recommend that Sangeeth engage in a deeper exploration of the literary world to gain further insights into modern English language, poetry, and its possibilities. Besides, I believe that life is not always pleasant and positive. In order to be a versatile, successful and memorable poet, Sangeeth must confront the darker aspects of human life, allowing him to incorporate a sense of postmodern reality into his work. I wish him more real-life experiences that will fuel his creativity and bring depth to his poetry.

– Dr. Syam Sudhakar

Blossoms: I Can Hear It

I can hear it
The humming and chirping,
Of birds in the morning.
Wow! said nature.

I can hear it
The tone of fishermen,
The happiness they have
While going back to their mothers.

I can hear it
The laughter of a baby
From the nearby house—
The ultimate mischief of God.

I can hear it
The cry of my cute white cat
From some faraway place.
Maybe Heaven? Yes, maybe.

I can hear it
The loud laughter of a madman
Walking down the street,
Praising not God, but life.

But no sound that I've heard
Has so much beauty
As, the colour of the sky
During sunrise, maybe.

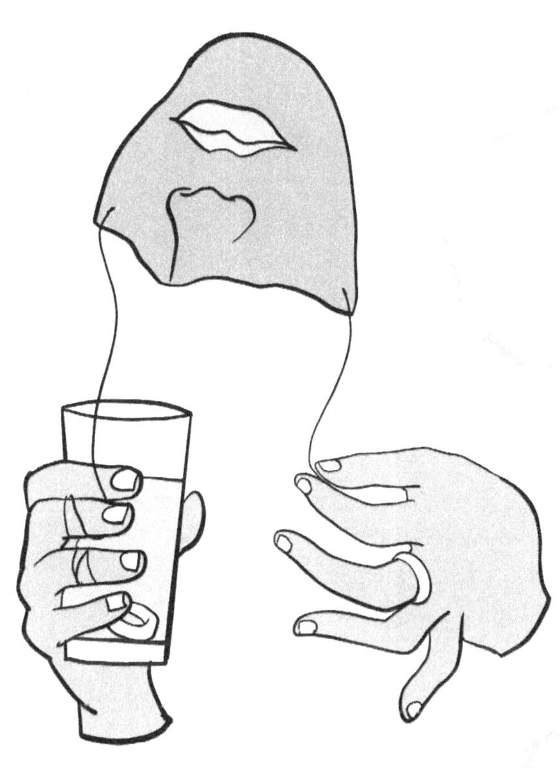

Illustrations: Devaprakash

Land of Fantasy

I saw it today also,
Her thin white hands
Having a ring with a cross
On her finger,
Which glows so bright.

When I tried to look at her face,
I couldn't see it,
As it was so bright.
"Oh! It's okay, get ready
And go to school."

On my way to school,
I saw a lady begging
For food in a shop.
It made me sad;
I rushed to her and gave my lunch.

When I heard my school bell ringing,
I started to run.
She gave back my lunch box
And waved with a smile.
I ran to school with a joyful heart.

During the afternoon,
I started to get hungry,
So I took my water bottle and drank—
It was something else,
But not water.

I drank it fully;
Thus, I filled my soul.
It was so tasty, and I thought
That was some new juice
Which Mom made.

After school, I looked for her,
But didn't see her.
Later, when I reached home
And came to the kitchen after my shower,
I heard Mom scream.

"Whose ring is this?"
I was shocked to see that too.
The same ring which
I saw in my dreams
Was inside my lunch box.

I was confused and told Mom,
"I don't know, Mom.
Anyway, your juice was really great."
Which made Mom murmur,
"Oh! What happened to my boy? What juice?"

The Man

The sun is my father,
The moon is my mother.
Though I see you every day,
I'm very far from you.
Distance is always the same,
But love goes on to change.
Sometimes we play hide and seek
With the help of clouds.
I play with firecrackers
In times of happiness
To make you enlightened.
At a young age,
I was afraid of darkness.
Though the sun was away at night,
The moon stood strong as hope.
As a grown-up,
The man jumped from inside
And was trying to be my father.
The light rays
That come through the branches
To my face seem scattered,
Yet gives a beautiful scene of me
To the world
That moves in a great rhythm!

Matter of Time

I was a kid
When I crawled from
The last bench to the middle.
It felt like a comedy
For my teachers,
But I crawled again and again.
My soul always needs more,
And thus, to reach first.
When in school,
I craved to move forward again,
From pencil to pen,
And then to fountain pen.
Later, when I started
To use the fountain pen,
I understood the power of the pencil,
As it was easier to erase.
The skills of the people around me
Were always a mystery.
I admired my father the most
When I was a kid.
Later, this mystery was also shattered
As time flew.
Now all these experiences
Made the real me
In a matter of time.

Bunker

Two in a bunker
And six in a room
Made it a chamber,
But never a gas chamber.

Morning was the time
Of actual battle,
When all the six
Compete to run away.

The chamber blossomed
Into a fairyland
As one stayed
To bring some light through words.

At night,
Again the fire burned too high
When all the six returned.
This made everyone melt.

Years passed;
Still, the chamber is the same.
The one who always stayed
Made the world thrill.

The words that rushed
From his mind to the world
Made his life
A story of millions.

Thus, the real conqueror
And the shining star
Went on to write
More and more.

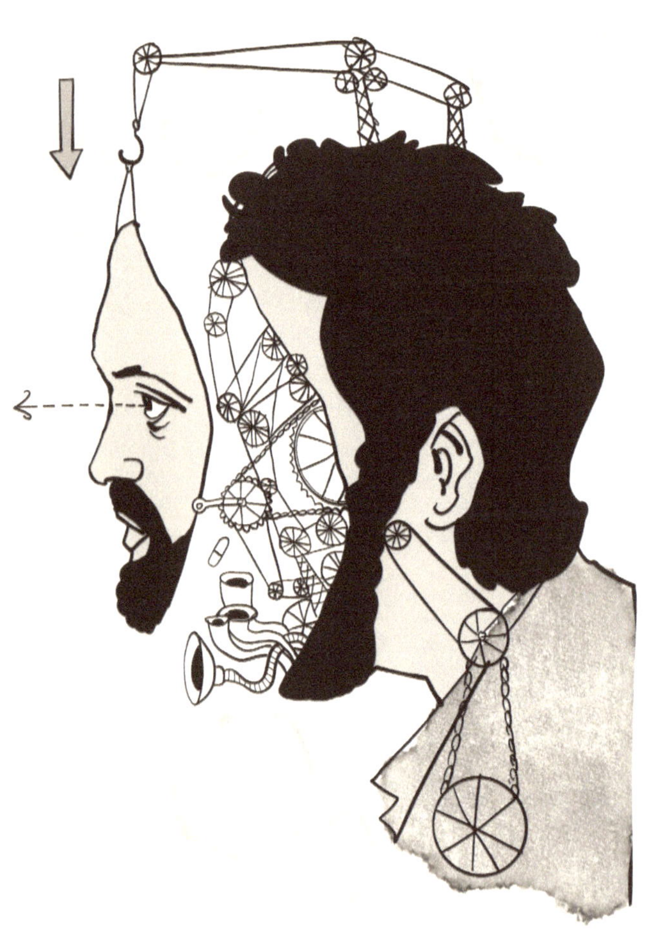

Autobiography

Moving ahead
And leaving everything behind,
But the smell of a chase rises.

Moving ahead of time
And making it
Just a number.

Moving ahead of centuries
And taking its
Veil of pride.

Moving ahead of the new
As some grey shades
Are spotted.

Moving ahead of inventions
As more interesting ones
Are discovered over time.

Moving ahead of deadly diseases
By finding medicines
And confirming their death.

Moving ahead of wounds
As healing is left
To willpower.

Moving ahead of human intelligence
As artificial ones arrive;
Now it's between them.

That smell is rising.
Yes, they are chasing me.
Now memories make me fall!

Ode to the Cuckoo's Song

Cuckoo's song made me weep;
That soothing voice
Pierced into my heart,
Made it wide open,
But no drop of blood.

Joy of the cuckoo,
The vibe it passes to nature,
Made me listen to its song carefully,
Which took me to
Ultimate enlightenment.

The song made
Other birds silent.
Even the breeze that came,
Evading the mist,
Didn't shake the bird.

Now I realize
The creative brilliance of God.
My thick-haired, serious cat
Is also her fanboy.
He looks at her with mouth wide open.

But once the cuckoo's song
Made me cry,
As it took me to profound insights.
Later, the bird left me
In deep sorrow as it flew away.

Nature again returned
To its previous mode,
Yet all are craving
For you, my dear
Divine soul!

Waiting for You

Your smile
Once made everything
Around you blissful.

Fragrance floats
In your words,
Which light our souls.

The body's beauty is melting
As the charm of your
Inner beauty glows.

Your loud worship
Of God made angels
Dance in joy.

Admired by many,
As the spirit inside
Burns high.

Nothing lasts forever
In this magical ring,
Not even blood relations.

You seemed to be
A divine hope,
Like a lily in His hands.

Later, the ring lost its power;
Hot winds carrying dust blew,
Thus hope dried slowly.

Now even the cactus starts
To rub with its thorns
And mocks at you.

When the door was opened,
A dove came down
And poured the water of life.

Our wait is over;
A new light
Made the ring more magical.

Life is Somewhere

Life flows fiercely like a river,
Yet sometimes
Blows soothingly like a breeze.
Life is somewhere far,
But not too far away.

The secrets hiding behind life
Is like a child hiding,
Covering her eyes with her tiny hands.
True beauty lies in this
Hiding nature of life.

Leading a beautiful life,
In one person's view,
May be a bad cup of coffee
In another's view.
How challenging it is to lead a life!

One may believe
He has hacked life,
But he may just be
Tripping or hallucinating,
By using something precious than gold.

Life may not have grown
From an idiot's tale,
Even after five centuries.
Yet the true meaning of life
Lies in gratitude.

Let gratitude not rest with
Those you hold dear;
Show it to everything
In this world and the outer world.
Thus, peace blossoms within your heart.

Life is somewhere far,
But not too far away.

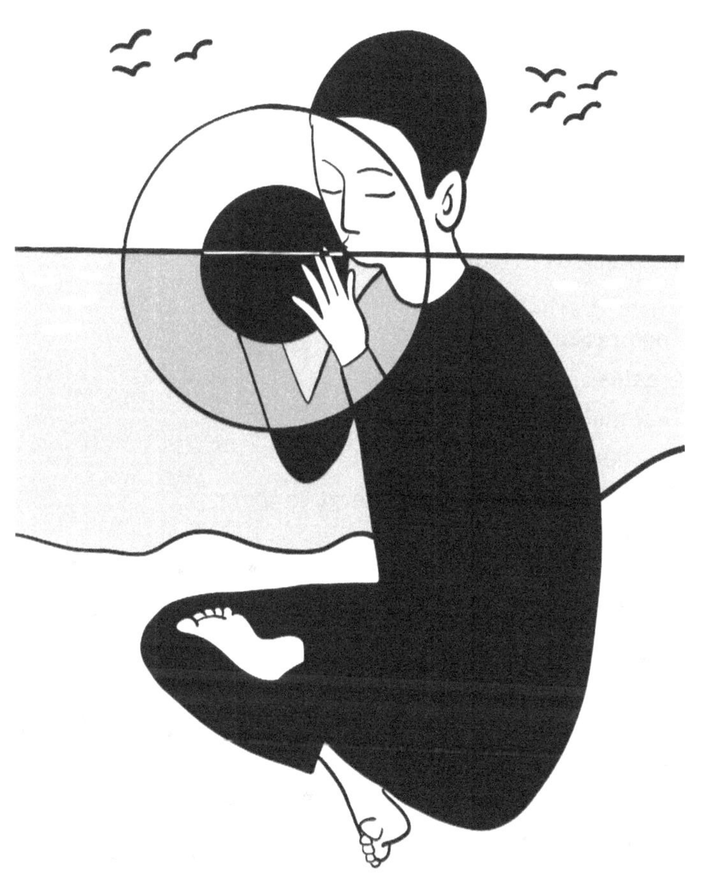

Ocean of Dreams

Breeze blowing from the ocean
Carries dreams of millions,
Spending their lives
In this vast, salty,
Yet precious treasure of Earth.

The pressure of dreams
Creates challenging waves
That make it hard
For the hunters.
Here, the breeze spreads energy to them.

Human willpower knows no bounds;
The champion is the mind,
Ready to fight and defeat the mammoth.
Thus, sail high above all
As a conqueror.

The Titanic was blown by ego,
Leading to a massive failure.
But it was not the end of dreams;
We learned from it
To dream even higher.

The fisher's trust
Allows them to collect
A boat full of love
From their mother ocean—
A loving family.

The worst challenge:
Pirates of the ocean
Make the treasure hunt
More adventurous.
Some pirates are even born in ocean!

There are many secrets
Hiding behind the ocean.
Dream high and sail
To uncover those hidden secrets.

The Blanket

Soothing blue colour
Makes the background rich;
Showers a cool look
On nature.
The beauty of everything
Projects in this nature's blanket.
Sometimes it changes the scene
To attract you more.
It seems like
Someone has hit some
Vivid watercolours on this blanket—
Maybe knowingly.
Oh! How beautiful!
It spreads some beauty
To the ocean too;
Thus, it makes the ocean its mirror.
Thanks rush high as vapours,
And the blanket floats.
Even the blanket
Purifies sunrays.
Rays are then
The definition of purity.
Yet the blanket doesn't mourn
For anything,
And gives its love as rain and snow,
Making nature a fairyland.

Crowned 7

Everyone has it.
Don't run behind
And make yourself sweat
Your entire life.
Search inside; it is within,
As you are born with it:
"The great King."
Victories and failures in each day
Load your crown with a feather
Which shapes and molds you
Into a more precious gem.
Make your next generation
Know this truth,
As your legacy
Safety transfers it to them,
So they are crowned too.
These precious feathers
May be lost
If you run behind
The fake glitters of this world.
So imprint this truth
Deeply in your heart,
Else a great fall may be seen.
Yet, being human,
Everyone is helpless,

As it is tough
To satisfy your thirst.
Many are still there to guide
And make you "King of Kings."
That will be your ultimate fall.
Just search
And find your destiny.
Make your life memorable,
Even for yourself.
Your birth is behind a plan;
Seek and rise high, achieving it.
At the time of crowning,
Your soul jumps
And flies high above the seven seas,
As you are being
Crowned by Him, the Ultimate!

Eclipse

Powerful glow of
350 vibrant full moons
Reflected on me
Deep from inside.

It woke me early in the morning,
But I can't see
That brightness
Anywhere in nature.

Everything is dull and gloomy.
As time passed,
It seemed like
The final day in paradise.

Hope inside is burning down
And pushed me
To a deep, narrow well,
Fully dark.

"Oh! God, why are you doing this?
Please save the world.
Where is the glow
Of 350 full moons?"

Slowly, I was going
To be unconscious.
My body went cold;
Hands started to shiver.

Finally, a ray of hope sprouted.
As I looked up,
I saw some light coming.
It made my soul jump with joy.

That was a new beginning—
The new bright light
Reformed everything
And had more glow than 350 full moons!

Complete

Now it's clear and still;
Peace floats everywhere.
Thus, mindfulness is attained,
And it's complete.
Those who travelled long are lucky,
But the world is sorry
For the unborn souls.
Unlucky, I guess.
Even the waves are still,
Which makes the ocean
A graveyard
Where dreams still live, though.
Now rivers and waterfalls
Never seek to travel more.
Weeds that grow on a tree
Once made it a bride,
Wearing precious jewels.
But those have fallen
And are gone too far away.
Everything is now
Covered in harmony.
This makes it complete.

Time Traveller

Am I actually here
Or somewhere else?
Doubt, which always
Scratches me.
Life is twirling
Inside a furious cyclone.
Oh! Is that a blessing
Or my life's luxury?
Thank you, Grandfather.
You are so grand.
What a great invention!
Yet why did you keep it
As a secret?
"500 BC to 2500 AD"—
What a fabulous work,
Yet never published.
Wireless charging was uncovered
When the telephone was not discovered.
A solution for air traffic block
By flying cars in 2200 AD
Makes me shocked.
I'm going for it
To explore and find the reason.
Oh God, what am I seeing?
Reality is mocking at me.

So grand, you knew it.
This machine will be the end of all.
You saved humanity;
Else it would be thrashed.
And you saved me too.
I know you are watching me
From somewhere near.
Let me just hide this safely.
But one doubt:
Am I actually here
Or still under my blanket?

Sorrow of a Pen

I was a champion;
My birth was much gifted
To his youthful hands!
Yet now?

In the beginning,
My words were sharp,
Thus entertains,
And make them think. Yet now?

I could not rest,
As thoughts made words
Flood like a river.
Yet now?

Even birds hummed to my lines;
Yes, I could hear it.
Those were the days of happiness.
Yet now?

Praises made me
Jump early in the morning,
And do magic with words till midnight.
Yet now?

Calm down, calm down;
Just safely land on Earth.
Come back! Don't fly so high!
Yet now?

My ego made it come early—
The one I never thought of,
But now I fear it the most.
Yet now?

Everything is fading;
No more words, though the ink is full—
A great fall of a century.
Yet now?

One last wish:
Make me a memory
When my words are flying high.
Yet now? "Now what? It's an end."

Lost Petal

Before the gift from heaven
Was perfect in my hands,
Now I've lost one petal
From that beautiful flower
Admired by many.

It lost its shape and pattern.
I fear the day
When I lose the rest.
My heart is mourning
For the lost one.

Not only me, but other admirers
And even the rest of the petals
Are also weeping for it.
Slowly, this sorrow
Spreads so deeply into nature.

I can't ask for another.
No, I don't need a new one,
But only pray for some miracle
To happen,
Thus to attain my lost gift.

Now the wind howls with fury,
And the rest of the flower
Drifted unconsciously
Somewhere.
It made me terrified.

I ran behind madly,
But it flew far and landed safely
In the hands of a Maharishi
Who's in deep meditation.
As I took the flower, I was shocked.

The lost petal sprouted;
The flower attained its beauty.
Oh! My lost one, you are back!

Mr. Perfect

"How are you doing?"
"Sometimes okay,
Sometimes bad,"
Mourned Mr. Perfect.

His mind flew
Up and down
As emotions
Boiled and froze.

At times he wore
The gown of an artist
Who was keen
To make everything perfect.

His life was perfect,
Like a straight line,
Though it seemed
To be a perfect circle.

Sometimes his mind
Floats calmly
Like a swan
That glides on a still lake.

But the swan was too rare
To be seen,
As mostly his mind
Clung to the nails of an eagle.

As the eagle flies madly
All around,
The life of a swan
Was just a dream too far.

At times he wore a mask
Of a master,
Wiser than the wisest,
Yet felt like a clown.

Master or clown?
Wise or fool?
Maybe a prank
By the Ultimate.

A prank not so rare,
As reality is truly weird.

Benevolence

Black is the purest.
Oh! Blacky, you are so pure.
Everything that shines
May make you dull,
Yet you remain exceptional.

Being nice to your
Loved ones seems good,
But you even share
Your meal with her,
Which you rarely get.

Some may call you
A bad omen.
Better they may
Fly to their world
Of only good omens.

You're a rose
That sprouted in a globe
That twirls in an
Everlasting turmoil,
My kind-hearted dear.

Your tail makes up
That of a hunter,
But your tail
Is an antenna that
Leads all species.

Make your way
And guide the world
To a new bright place.
Thus, crawl deep into
The limits of this universe.

Lotus Left

Floating like a lotus
In a tranquil lake,
It puts my mind at ease.
Though it felt amazing,
My soul got stagnant
As the lake was still.

I saw more like me
As time passed
In an always serene lake.
I felt no grief here,
Since I had some company,
But that made me love myself.

I was tough
And bold like a rock,
Thus hanging immaculately
In this lake of life.
Many lived here,
Facing their fate.

Only something like fish
Made some vibrations
In this otherwise
Always calm lake.
Here, the rain caused gentle ripples,
Though very few.

My destiny would be like others
If I never tried to come out.
So I dreamt always
And gave all my effort.
Thus, in the end,
I reached my true home.

The Supreme

Oh! My dear,
Much overwhelmed
And mad in your presence,
It actually took me
To another world.

You are not just a lily,
But something more.
Your shade
And perfect figure
Attract me deeply.

"But, my lily, where is your smell?"
"Oh! So you're only a fake lily,
But I don't feel any difference."
Beauty is chased by most,
And you're being chased.

Attracted by your beauty,
I got you from a boy
Who sells flowers.
I will never leave you,
My dear love.

You filled my soul,
Though you're purely
A crafted soul.
Godly skill reflects on you
As your charm goes on and on.

"To Happen"

A loud voice
Made everything start,
Turned the first chapter,
And taught us to dream high.
But take some time even to dream;
Thus, make it true—
Else it won't last long.

Even He took six days,
Which made it last so long.
Dreams are like tiny sticks
That fall from the tree of dreams.
Take time and feel it;
Dream many
To make a nest of life.

Some may laugh at you
For being carriers of stick.
Failures may bring you down,
Yet the decision is yours
To make your juice bitter or sweet.
These failures and laughs
Make it even sweeter.

Dream more
And make wings for your nest
To fly all around and do wonders.

Rising High

Make aims, not blames.
Aim high and go for one;
Makes it an easy catch.
Running, running behind many
Ends up with life running.

Her good eyes
Wish for our success more.
Maybe her son is great,
But she prays for us
With her beautiful eyes wide open.

Failures and failures come;
Just accept
And grab success.
Your fate is your carving—
Make it beautiful, not blame.

Words are sharp like arrows;
The beauty lies in its magic.
As it travels all around the world,
Its beauty does not fade
And lasts till mankind ends.

If you're ready to face life's bitter truths,
To embrace its hardships,
And experience other faces of loved ones,
Cut your wings of freedom,
Thus, discover your true self.

Running, running behind many
Ends up with life running,
Yet adventurous and reveals the real you.
Thus, the carvings made by you
Will have an Eternal touch!

Search for Paradise

Where is it?
Morning view of the river
From a mountain covered with
Tiny grass and mist makes it.

Where is it?
Having breakfast with your
Loving family, even if it's only
Bread and butter makes it.

Where is it?
Fishermen waving with a warm smile
To their family when going fishing,
Neglecting the hot afternoon sun makes it.

Where is it?
A stunning scene of kids
Running and jumping with joy
To their parents after school makes it.

Where is it?
Lovers walking in the park
In the evening,
Sharing their dreams makes it.

Where is it?
The praying and thanking sounds
Rising from houses
To the Creator makes it.

That was the end
Of a day in Paradise!
Oh! Where is it?

The Kingdom

Before I thought
Both are here only
In this world itself.
I always told my sister,
Who prays constantly to God,
To reach there,
That both are here only.
If you don't find it here,
Then you'll never see it!
As, death is an end.

Better seek and find it here;
Don't wait for more
And make your soul
Desperate at the end.
Life went fast and far;
My thoughts were crushed
As time passed.
Life pushed me down always,
Showed me only one—
The Kingdom ruled by Satan.

Hardships made me live
As a member of His Kingdom.
I didn't see anything
Soothing for my eyes,
Nothing that glows is precious.
I didn't see any glitters, too—
Even fake ones.
The breeze never blew;
I saw only wind carrying dust.
My heart mourned deeply.

They hit me with ropes
Having thorns,
Which made me unconscious.
They gave me just water,
Which I bite and drink.
These made me finally trust Him.
Now I hope to see Him
And live in His Kingdom
After my death in this hell.
"Thus, his soul met Him!"

No More Caged

No more caged;
Though the bars are seen,
It feels so light—
Only to make me
Not forget my past.

Now I'm flying long,
Like a patriotic bird,
Floating freely like a feather
Around the world,
Seeking and exploring all hidden!

The world once felt so small,
As I was inside mine.
Now I've started to dig deeply
So I can slide into it
And make life a reason to explore.

No more old wine
That clouds my mind;
I crave the sweetness
Of mountain honey—
Pure, untouched, and free.

No more a puppet,
Chained by fake friends;
My mind seeks pleasure
That comes from connecting
With peaceful souls.

The road ahead is clear;
I may have covered
Half the way.
Life has taught me the value
Of true freedom, and I rejoice!

Endless

The sky seems brighter than usual.
Change is spreading over
Other things too,
But not in humans.
They are the same, living in cages.

Chasing, chasing a fleeting dream,
Earning, earning to feed generations,
Yet, never satisfied,
Praying to work their sixth sense,
But they may loose their current one.

Dreaming high,
Flying high,
Failing though,
No value for relations—
Value is for worldly matters.

Seniors are weeping
In old age homes;
Juniors are tied in boarding schools.
The middle are the rope pullers of cages—
So they are safely caged too!

No time to love,
No time to smile;
The century is going down,
Again and again,
Measured on the scales of time.

God knew this,
Thus created man the last;
Else life could have seen
Its end before.
Yet they think it is endless.

Yes, it is,
But just pause and look
As the sky seems brighter than usual.

Little One

Vibrant little one,
Covered in blood,
Came to their hands
As a dream.
Cry, cry, baby's cry—
Took them to a new state.
Vibe of positivity,
Made everything swing.
Yet the universe clung
To the cradle
As the baby cried deeply.
Nature moved on
To deep grief,
Thus got stuck in an orbit,
No way to move on
From this sighing plight.
Later, the time came;
A new wave reached the shore.
The baby fell deep into it,
A new dream flashed
With vivid scenes
And brought the baby peace,
Which the baby had mourned for.

Ecstasy in Love

Love doesn't make you alone;
Thus, I strive
To love everything,
Though hard I try.

Ecstasy in love
Makes me addicted to you.
My love, you are precious—
Stay close and satisfy the fire inside.

Meeting and spending time
With you is my Sukrita!
My life is at its fullest
When I'm with you.

You are my ecstasy,
The most beautiful sight,
Your beauty is shining like
The North Star's guiding light.

Fire is burning high;
During the shower, I see it—
Vapour, vapour moving high,
Never a mere miracle.

"Why are you blabbering?"
"Oh, no, Mom, don't wake me up!
 Let me just finish this."
"No, it's over; see you later."

Goan Tragedy: Anjuna

I

Anjuna opens it,
Your mind and soul,
Truly opens your third eye.
Stepping on the sand
Makes your body move in a trance.
Dark rocks on the beach
Have made Anjuna a dark beauty.

I I

During sunset, the sky seems
Like a painting,
A gift for the world.
As people around the globe
Hold their hands here,
But it's not a paradise anymore—
The other side is really dark.

I I I

Natives knew this
But are helpless.
People get wiped off
As one seen in this season
Is not seen later.
This makes them
Forget to smile.

IV

Revolvers are always loaded.
Here is an easy trick:
Better close your eyes tight.
Hey, the time has come to act.
Now open your eyes wide
And make it a paradise again.
Tiny old ashes are good for a new start.

V

Once I met an Austrian lady
From Anjuna.
She asked me, "How's life?"
I replied, "Good. How's yours?"
She replied, "It's been so good."
The vibe of old Anjuna lies here.
Thou art always in the creamy layer!

When I Saw You

When I first saw you,
I was in a desperate mood,
But your presence
Slowly changed my mood.
When you stood by my side,
It felt like
I had seen you somewhere before.
Your smile flashed me
Into some past memory—
Maybe a past life.

Everything is changing;
My thoughts upon marriage
Are changing now, as I saw you.
Before, I thought of devoting my life
To something that is my destiny.
"It's God's will; she is for you,
Thus you achieve your destiny,"
Someone murmured.
That voice was similar
To the voice that comes in my dreams.

When she was going away,
I rushed to her
And expressed my feelings.
A smile was the answer, and she told me,
"I appreciate your guts; I'm impressed."
Thus, marriage happened,
And we started to live together.
Everything was going like
Someone else's plan—
It felt strange.

Happiness reached its heights
When a baby girl was born.
Later, when the baby started to talk,
I realized the truth
With goosebumps all over my body:
That voice which murmured
And I heard in my dreams
Is my baby's voice!
When I looked at her in shock,
She smiled with a wink.

Hope: Gift for the Future

Still, some hope is left.
Oh! Where is it?
Look closer, as it is fading;
Some tiny pearls still exist.

Still, some hope is left.
The Earth is moving with it.
Even rain is a hope for life,
As nature gets thrilled within.

Still, some hope is left.
Birth marks a new beginning
In the universe; so angels dance,
Like peacocks dancing in the rain.

Still, some hope is left.
Prayer always has an answer.
A great ray of hope was given
Two thousand years ago, a gift for the future.

Still, some hope is left.
Priests and Sannyasis,
Who devote their lives to others,
Are certainly a beam of hope.

Still, some hope is left.
The cry of a baby is a hope—
That baby hopes for food,
Or for someone to wipe away its fear.

Still, some hope is left.
Fire poppies hopes to rise
From ashes, and they truly do,
To become an ultimate beauty.

Still, some hope is left.
To move the world forward.
Hope sprouts like a flower,
Spreading the fragrance of life!

The Fire

Those glorious wings
With fire came down again.
I can see that glow
In my eyes.
The glow was truly heavenly.
Wings with fire taught me
God is real.

I came upstairs
To the window,
As the sound made by the doves
At the window seemed so sweet.
Doves murmured to nature,
Thus creating an anointing vibe
That made everything fall into a trance.

The joy never lasted too long,
As the undergrounds were opened,
And evils came with more energy
To thrash this happiness.
Now the game began.
Pressure flew high
As the fight went on and on.

Finally, the Ultimate
Showered His power.
Thus darkness slowly
Faded and faded into a shadow!

83

Season of Blames

Thus the world was created
With vivid seasons.
It makes a change,
And helps Him escape from boredom.

Yet they made it
A reason to blame.
When summer makes it hot,
They mourn for rain.

When it rains
And nature bursts with joy,
That soothing smell of soil rises,
But now they call for the next.

Watching their changing needs,
He became angry.
Thus, He hits the sky so hard
And makes thunderstorms.

It made them frightened,
Thus He decided to fold the chart
And close the door of seasons.
This thrashed the balanced rhythm!

Now everything came as they wished.
This ended up in a great mess.
"We can call Him," someone said.
Thus, prayers rise up to the sky.

Later, He opened the door again,
Yet they were the same,
Crawling with their dreams,
Calling and making blame on Him.

But this just made Him
Smile and whisper, " Poor folks."

All of a Sudden

Everything happened
All of a sudden,
And now I'm here,
Alone in a room,
Sentenced to a life term
In this prison,
Though I stand pure,
Innocent as dawn.
Here, I don't see any reason
To praise God,
So I spend time cursing.
Days passed,
But very slowly,
Dragging me
Into a boredom profound,
A solitude understood
Only by the most wretched souls.
"Why was I born to this fate?"
Life is still moving ahead on,
An endless journey.
I can't see any diseases, too.
Why doesn't a deadly disease
Choose my body?
Even they have left me alone.
Thinking all this

Makes me suffocate.
I need a change.
So I wrote a letter
To my mother,
Describing my innocence,
As I need to be a fine man
Only in front of her.
The jailer took it and posted,
The letter of innocence.
Again, days passed,
Yet time still crawls slowly.
My heart ached for her reply.
Finally, her letter came,
A soft snowfall
In my desert-like mind.
"Don't be sad, stay strong.
I will fight for you.
Let truth win."
The reply from my mother
Showered me with positivity
And made me love God,
A spark in the dark.

Nowhere

I went above everything,
Flashed back and forth,
Tried hard to be in the now,
Failed, though.
Mostly, I'm somewhere dreamed by many,
As I stay close to nowhere,
Riding in a time machine
To the past through my memories.
But the future is safe in my dreams.
Many questioned me, "Why?"
"Live in the present."
Tough, though.
Look at nature,
Feel the breeze,
Make your soul free.
Thus, indulge in the joy
Of being in the now.

Ode to a Mayfly

Time is beyond,
And we are blessed.
As we have it more,
We give it less care.
Someone once wrote,
Time waits for no one;
Life may have gone far
When we gain this insight.
This morning, a visitor
Came to my bed on a swift wind:
A mayfly
With broken wings,
Fighting against
The universe's most deadly truth: death.
As the mayfly now looks
Face to face with death,
Our Mother Earth
Stands by its side.
This brings relief
To the fly.
Though at the beginning
It lives for a year
In the water,
The poor mayfly has only
One day's life in the air,

And I witness its end now.
I tried to make it fly,
But the poor soul seemed
Lost upon my bed.
The scene looked like
Nature was giving a goodbye
To this unfortunate fellow.
I wish that soul a brighter rebirth
In the future!

Dancing Legends

On a warm summer day,
Shakespeare walks
Down a narrow road,
Where lilacs bloom
On either side,
Making the path
Into a purple garden,
With the fresh fragrance
Of lilac in the air.

He walks to the funeral
Of a dear friend,
Holding a bouquet of marigolds
Close to his chest.
As he reaches the church
And stands by the body,
His heart beats high.
Though he tries to hold back the tears,
He breaks down in sorrow.

On his way home,
He decides to visit the writers club,
Hoping to overcome his desperate mood.
Inside, five legends dance,
Whiskey glasses in hand,
Calling to him, "Bard of Avon, welcome!"
In the corner, Eliot sits,
Reading a book on critical thought—
Yet it is a room of joy.

Later, the dance comes to an end.
Keats and Fanny,
The youngest among them,
Are sharing their love.
Keats declares,
"My dear Minxtress, thou art my bright star."
The others leave them alone,
Leaving them in their world,
As the Bard smiles at their bliss.

Then Eliot breaks his silence,
Approaching Shakespeare with words,
"Life is very long when one considers
The amount of time spent in waiting.
What's your opinion, Mr. Bard?"
Shakespeare replies, in a low voice,
"That's why I say, life is a tale told by an idiot,
Full of sound and fury, signifying nothing."
Eliot raises a glass, "Let's toast to nothingness."

www.ingramcontent.com/pod-product-compliance
Lightning Source LLC
Chambersburg PA
CBHW022036150726
47990CB00002B/991